ZOO

THIS
COLORING
BOOK
BELONGS TO :

....

LION FAMILY

GIRAFFE

MONKEY

CHIMPANZEE

KANGAROO

GAZELLE

PANDA

PENGUIN

BEAR

CHEETAH

TIGER

OSTRICHES

ZEBRA

CROCODILE

CAMEL

RABBIT

HIPPOPOTAMUS

RHINO

SQUIRREL

DUCKS

EAGLE

PARROT

DOLPHIN

SHARK

OWL

TAPIR

HYENA

KOALA